MEASURELESS SILENCE:
Poems of the Wild and the West

poems by

CHRISTINE MULVEY

Finishing Line Press
Georgetown, Kentucky

MEASURELESS SILENCE:
Poems of the Wild and the West

For my parents: Irene and Diarmuid

Copyright © 2021 by CHRISTINE MULVEY
ISBN 978-1-64662-680-9 First Edition
All rights reserved under International and Pan-American Copyright Conventions. No part of this book may be reproduced in any manner whatsoever without written permission from the publisher, except in the case of brief quotations embodied in critical articles and reviews.

Publisher: Leah Huete de Maines

Editor: Christen Kincaid

Cover Art: Christine Mulvey

Author Photo: Jack Kuehn

Cover Design: Elizabeth Maines McCleavy

Order online: www.finishinglinepress.com
also available on amazon.com

Author inquiries and mail orders:
Finishing Line Press
PO Box 1626
Georgetown, Kentucky 40324
USA

Table of Contents

Fir Ridge 1
Evening in Yellowstone 2
Buffalo Watch 3
Entering Montana 4
Eastern Montana 5
Glacier Park 6
Garden Wall 7
Two Medicine Lake 8
Dusty Star 9
Bear Country 10
The Beartooths 11
Caught 12
Passage 14
Roadkill 15
Stovepipe Canyon 16
Blackfeet Winter 17
Solitude 18
Camp Fire 19
In Missoula 20
Teach Us 21
Stalking 22
Dark Mercy 23
Thanksgiving 25
After the Storm 26
Visiting the Doctor in a Fly Over State 27
Reno Dreaming 28
A Different Kind of Spring 29
California Sunday, Late July, 2014 30
Unsettled 31
In the City 32

WHAT DO YOU LOVE, YOU ASKED.
TELL ME—EVERYTHING!

AND SO, I ANSWERED:
I LOVE EVERYTHING

THAT'S WILD—ALL WE DO NOT,
ALL WE CANNOT YET CONTROL,

EVERYTHING UNCAPTURED,
UNDEFILED,

ITS OWN, ORIGINAL SELF,
MERCURIAL

AND RAW—ALL THAT CANNOT BE,
THAT STILL REFUSES

TO BE
TAMED.

FIR RIDGE

Come with me, out to where the soft round shapes
of the fallen snow lie draped across the bushes, like the thighs
and hips of a sleeping god curled up on the open bedspread of the land.

Here willow twigs stand frozen, furred by hoar
and under the diamond glint of the bowl of night the river,
black as molten pitch, whispers underneath its skin of ice.

In the silence, only an occasional flumpf of snow
falling from bare boughs, tinkling the air, or the mournful
honking of the swans calling from the lake the whole night through.

Here, tell me the story of your lonesomeness, your unheard prayers!
And I will show you how, underneath that ridge, inked like a koan
across this boundless white, a solitary bison ploughs his head

in big, slow sweeps from side to side
knowing that six feet down
there must be grass.

EVENING IN YELLOWSTONE

Light spreads low across the wide Lamar
slides down from peak to hill to lea

down to where shale swales mark the river
and a stand of cottonwood

burns, shivering and dark beneath
the tawny bowl of sky.

Behind a swathe of sage, beyond those
swaying grasses,

right beside that gliding
line of water

the Druid Pack
is gathering.

BUFFALO WATCH

In this vast expanse of winter—white earth,
white light, white sky, the very air itself
white with cold, shaggy with snow

the silent pines, the black, eternal river
stitched by ice into the mirror of the sky—
you stand in the sliding water

your swaying head snow-spattered
from the search for food, your muscled tongue
twitching, your dark all-knowing eye watching

me watching you, guarding you. My tiny image
caught inside its glistening, as though you'd
taken me and all the fretfulness I carry

and pressed me deep
inside yourself for safe
and sacred keeping.

ENTERING MONTANA

The widest skies are here to greet me, white with early sun,
the road, a scar across the sleeping animal of the land,

beckoning forever. And across forever—not a building,
not a sound. Only the rush of wind as my car slides through,

pancakes and eggs in my stomach, the smell of sage
rising with the sun, washing my senses clean.

The slow, unblinking mountains already underneath
their dust of snow, their forests suedeing the hills,

a line of cottonwoods yellowing the satin chord of the river.
Across the valley floor no fence, no ditch, no stone.

Only the waving hair of the limitless prairie.
And high above it all the green white lance of lightning.

EASTERN MONTANA

Leaving the surging mountains far behind
the land spills out and out again beneath skyscapes that scatter
shadows like small scraps of skin dropped from the raptor's beak.

Here where seas once sighed, the lilt of light
across the wide horizon paints soft palomino shades of prairie
folding fields, one into the other, while space and silence sing

the constant movement of the wind
parting the grasses' tresses, shivering the streams, lifting
the large lax wing of the eagle's gliding. Here, the land's a line,

an edge from which the sky
has sprung, a broken shell discarded, holding its secrets
close and one must kneel, nose to ground, to feel the tracks

of rain-drops etched
into the dried-out earth like lines upon a lovers' palm,
to see the prints of feet, of wings, the fins of tiny things;

and water, caught between the crevices of stone—
mud-holes, rock-bowls, sand-folds—poised in the cushioned
leaves of sage, each drop counted; each drop held; feeding the

mystery of the
moon-rose, pink and pale
against the dung-grey dirt.

GLACIER PARK

Always it is the highest peaks that draw me—
those knife-sharp ramparts etched against the sky:

Reynolds, Oberlin and Little Chief.
Dusty Star and Mahatopa.

Wrapped in cloud. Stung by rain.
Ice-shorn. Sun-polished,

pumping their muscle
into this air I'm breathing.

I see them huddling neck deep, sunk in snow,
furred by silence, these *Shining Mountains,*

Backbone of the World, their blades of red
and green and grey that once lay undersea,

soft and molten, feeding the gaping mouths
of creatures that now gaze back at them

through me.

GARDEN WALL

I think of it in winter—
sharp whine of wind, the cold's long blade
merciless.

The sun's thin gold today
burning through the turquoise ice,
the snow's mauve breath

curling upwards from its bones.
And I am drawn—as moth to flame—
to feel that burn

to reach, to soar, to fly beyond
the Garden Wall, to call the fearsome wrap
of wilderness back there

my home.

TWO MEDICINE LAKE

Walking onto the frozen lake
beneath these chiseled mountains,
snow puff-powdering the purple air,

ravens rustling by, carrying light
like a drink in the curve of their backs,
the ragged cry of their cackling

deepening the thrum of silence:
I am a pine seed stuttering
onto a stainless platter,

the air around me
color of bluebirds' feathers
twirling into an ocean of sky.

DUSTY STAR

High above your wrap of forest up you rise.
Stone cliffs buttered by the moon, gored by
glaciers, bear-roamed, sung to by the wolves.

Pillar of marble, haughty with ice, steel rain,
hard shine, the silver necklace of the night
caught in the nets of your trees,

towering over the purpled lake, your image
shivering in its depths, leaning in, as stars
lean towards the Earth, beckoning.

BEAR COUNTRY

Stopped by the burning thigh of mountain
the flickering grass betrays the river
buried in the crawling marsh.

By the fox's den the cougar's print waits
underneath old leaves left by the
snow's soft creeping.

Down from the ridge at the water's edge
the wet trail trembles. Aspen stir, white
barks bleeding from the clawing.

A mile from camp, exhausted, we feel it—
the eye of the bear dropping
from our backs.

THE BEARTOOTHS

For hours I've walked
through towering canyons,
roaring stone,

stood on rushing
hillsides watching granite peaks
spit shy

and awesome water,
all around me walls of mist,
the sound of cracking

rock, the slow inexorable
demise of boulders—and this sky,
unfathomable,

thundering
with magnificent
indifference.

CAUGHT

Out I went
wet of nose,
gleam of eye,
eardrums full
of panting,
to paw my way
across the hills
ankle deep in duff
pulsing with
the body-smell
of earth.
Wind gathering
in the folded forest
scuffling among
the broken branches
fingering needles
orange cones
bark flaring
with the spit
of ice and suddenly,
it's snowing!
White waves of
air letting down
slow curtains
all around me.
Now the light
folds over
and is gone.
In the loamy dark
the woods
turn black.

No pelt
against the storm,
heartbeats skittering,
fear locked
in the corners
of my eyes,
I turn for home,
rampant and feral
no longer
what I want
to be…

PASSAGE

Having skied all day down powdery roads
past forest-darkened slopes, frozen-air-burn in our lungs,

clucklikling of snow-black streams coiling and shadowy
beneath their case of ice, we stop to watch a herd of deer

watch us. Behind them on the eastern sky the Crazies
shine like milk. Ear flickers. Eye quivers. The Earth breathes in,

and out, and silence
drops its cloak.

Then one by one they cross the road, step by tiptoed step,
delicate and shy, to climb the bank beyond

where suddenly they lift their legs and leap
into a sky of pink and orange.

ROADKILL

When they found you, unexpected,
in the doe's dead flesh

you were perfect—spotted back,
tender neck, tiny pointed feet,

your thin skin matted and red,
smooth and sticky with the skein

of womb—your soon-to-be life
snuffed out.

They wanted to dump you
so we carried your tiny corpse

through thigh-deep snow,
three women guided by the sound

of melting water, swirl
of wind drawing the evening

clouds over
the throbbing skies.

We folded you and laid you down
snug between the roots of firs

rocking your unborn soul
back into the matted fur of Earth,

smoking our prayers, chanting and
singing, as women do,

reluctantly, painstakingly
sending you home.

STOVEPIPE CANYON

Beneath these trees
tall as watchtowers
sunk into red dirt
made of their flesh—
great sloughed-off layers
of themselves—curved flanks of bark
moss rugs old leaves twig-bits and mushrooms—
blood-dark cream-thick flecked tin
big as dishes small as fingertips
poking through the
fruited ground.
Birds screech.
A squirrel cackles.
Insects come and go.
And I pass by
tiny, fleeting,
folding myself
through this mulch
of aeons feeding
from this forest table
heaving with sun-
buttered slabs of
silence—
Everything
food for
the Holy
that hangs
like wings
of gauze
in the
edge
-less
air.

BLACKFEET WINTER

In the feral silence of this place,
the Earth and everything upon it
seems to hum—

one high-pitched, seamless note—
the solitary and unbroken
sound of lonely.

Nothing like the black and white
of winter to scare the ghosts
of unremembered wounds

to light; bring my true face—naked
as in death—before me to splinter,
like jack frost on this window pane,

whatever thoughts I have
of self, security
or significance.

SOLITUDE

Beside me
the formless lamplight spills.

Small cracks
in the dark glass mapping

the forgotten shape
of home.

Mountains fling their lonely light.
The evening

fills with a plangent yelping.
Across the prairie

colors lose their lines
and bleed away.

Night grows
huge and empty—

measureless the silence
opening around me.

CAMP FIRE

In the whispering heat we sit,
sharp crack of the cold at our backs.

Between us a ringing silence
fed with the meat of berries and wild deer.

Across the flames
your eyes, inscrutable.

Below, where your best friend's wife lies
dying, the raucous city weaves its shroud of promises.

Here, hard moon on a lonesome lake.
Stunned hills logged and littered. A sky of stars

and the wind's swan song
soaring.

IN MISSOULA

Here the paths do not receive my step,
the walls do not make way.

Beyond the glare of neon lights
I search the sky for one small

patch of dark—untouched
by humans.

Hemmed in I break
like rotten wood

like the trunks of trees
long dead,

flaking into the forest floor
crumbling back to earth.

Would that I could in my breaking
pour my powder on the ground,

feed my memories to the soil,
feed the seeds that sleep there

dreaming of their journey
towards the clouds.

But I am numb and empty,
hard as these city streets,

wordless as the quilt of forest
I remember on the mountains' flank,

dead as the burned-out snag
harsh against the evening's silk

where no bird yet
has perched.

TEACH US

How can I know myself—
my kind—until I've seen you,

walked inside your skin,
padded the earth naked to the whip of wind,

scratch and tear of bramble, taste of
blood, the ever-present lure of danger?

You who run in packs, noses to the dirt,
long-legged in the gathering night;

you who walk alone, fire of your muscle
rippling your furs, leaving the marks

of your claws on the furrowed trunks
of trees and mountains;

you who move in herds,
your seamless breathing steaming the air,

your ancient and slow-motioned
flows darkening the hills—

how can I know myself—
my kind—until I've been you?

What will be lost forever
when you're gone?

STALKING

All day the clouds bent down to spread their hair
across the hills, their soft white light French-kissing
all those secret curves.

Now we lie hidden in the raffia of prairie,
the day's last wind a shuddering in our ears.

Yards away a herd of elk staring,
holding their breath as we hold ours,
lowering their bodies to the ground

to lie sphinx-like and watch the hills
turn color into scent and disappear.

Now the luscious moon comes out,
blue light like snow in twilight, silence
pounding down, beat by steady beat.

Like children, like the elk, we lie
nuzzling the ground.

In our nostrils, the mother smell.
In our eyes, the stare
of ancestors.

DARK MERCY

There it is: thin trickle of darkness oozing
from one nostril, dripping into the grass.

Your long white head, slender, twitching,
ears laid back across your muscled neck.

Loose dewlaps of your throat beating
like the wings of a frantic bird.

Faint spots on your fur like spattered stars
fallen from the mercy of the sky—

How can I leave you?

Beside us the ice-green hair of the river combing
past, a small wind setting the cottonwoods

shivering, pushing bruised clouds over
the quiet grace of the mountains.

Saturday night after the pubs—
too many cars, too close, too fast—

You didn't stand a chance.

Who left you like a bunch of twigs, tossed
onto the highway by a gust of wind?

Who left your babies like two, used
tooth-picks snapped and broken,

like butterflies trodden into the pitch.
I think of how I take and toss the petals of my life

no notion of the treasures I've been given.

When I kneel beside you your front legs try to kick,
flap and paw the ground but find no purchase.

Could your nose be any more gorgeous,
your eyes more desperate,

your tiny hooves, sharp as oyster shells,
any more exquisite?

Around us, Time slows to the Eternal.
Your pale heart thunders on.

Pushing through the bowing grasses
to the car, I fetch my knife,

push back, kneel to touch you one last time,
humming the "Gate":

Gate, Gate, Paragate, Parasamgate. Bodhi swaha.

Kick of hoof against my palm.
Tiny sound of your throat skin

tearing. Hot blood spurting.
Dark eyes milking.

Your shoulders heaving,
meeting the curve of my palm

as it strokes the rough, sad satin
of your hide,

one last time.

TRAVELLING FOR THANKSGIVING

*I'm not cutting maple leaves out of pastry
to hand-dip in chocolate just for show—
I mean, WHO has time for that?*

*And I'm not taking days off work
so I can cook for everyone—my friends
do that. I think they're crazy.*

*Mom's in detention and Dad—
he's in the Vets Home now
near where we used to live,*

*five hundred miles from here.
Since the economy tanked,
I see them only once a year—*

*Travelling—
that's how I spend
the holidays!*

*I miss those hills, I do. I miss the lake,
the drive up past the timberline,
the way the air smells there.*

*Dad says it makes you reverent—
all them mountains, the river
in the canyon shining,*

*the lake—all that water
right there in the middle
of the desert.*

AFTER THE STORM

Grey beach of my driveway pocked by paws,
rippled with pine, shorn locks of fir

scissored by wind, twig bits, acorns
smeared on the rust-colored clay.

The glass orb of the sky blown thin by defeat
tinkling with the sound of braiding waters.

Last night's storm a stun of wildness.
Animals cowering. Stars crackling.

Wind slashing at the white hair of the moon
as it fell brokenly through the trees.

Now the sun unwraps the air
like cellophane unfolded,

lifts the bare flesh of morning
into the skies—how I need

the blue suede shadow that is hovering now
underneath the barren trees.

VISITING THE DOCTOR IN A FLY OVER STATE

We drive the forgotten malls—nail parlors, hair salons,
storefronts flashing Payday Loans, Discount Liquor, Porn.
McDonalds, Dennys, Subway, Motel 6 and 8, Dollar Tree,
Les Schwab, Chevron, Shell—

Nobody here ever wants espresso.

Casino signs in the noonday sun, an Indian Grandma
rolling her wheelchair up the wrong side of the highway.
In the distance empty houses reaching towards the snow-
smeared hills, their piled-up roofs the color of sun-killed harvests.

In the doctor's room *People Magazine, Sports Illustrated,
Readers Digest*. On the cover of *Rifleman*, a white man rages.
Outside the window by the outsized trucks, an old man totters
past, leading his wife, her hands wrapped tight in bandages—

Nobody here is under fifty.

RENO DREAMING

In the dark casinos, women in bunny suits, brown tights,
cleavages deep as sand dunes, scurry through the crowds of men.

Everywhere glitz and bling, like makeup on an older woman,
and the tinkle of the chandeliers stirring the smoke-stained air.

In the windowless pit gamblers in Goodwill clothing
smoke and stare—eyes flat, faces the color of gravel.

Outside, the hills are floury with snow, great mounds of dough
splotched by sage like carcasses under the waning sky.

A wind blows chip bags through Walmart's lot.
Across the highway an aging vet, his sleeping bag leaking feathers,

pushes his cart past Lender signs, thrift stores, vape joints.
Above his head an arrowed flock of geese wing by.

At the porn shop by the liquor store, he stops and stares—
flimsy g-strings, bits of bras, naughty in pink and black—

only a sup of whiskey or a boozy dream
in a cold night's sleep, away.

A DIFFERENT KIND OF SPRING

Prickly from summer heat in April
I prowl the hills and the febrile silences

of pine and oak, scotch broom,
bay laurel, manzanita.

Yesterday our road was closed
by one magnificent ponderosa

pulled from its dust
by thirst.

Today the iron of the sun lies
heavy on its shoulders,

shadows of vultures, dark
against the paling needles,

my dog pulling at its branches
tossing great slabs of its brittle bark

into the crackling air—
Everywhere,

the smell of a land
rain has forgotten.

CALIFORNIA SUNDAY, LATE JULY, 2014

Stuck in traffic heading west on 80
back to the city.

Outside the window raffia fields,
necklaces of cars strung out in all directions,

coastal mountains hazed
with smoke, dust, pesticide.

It's ninety-six degrees.

At the station where I stop for gas, smells
of fast food, spilt oil, dried pee. I start the pump.

Inside a TV flickers: rockets thump,
tear through family rooms and hospitals.

A man runs through the burning
air, looking for the second half

of his daughter.

Last night, I stared into the space
between the stars—

up there a universe of fire, gasses spitting
colors into the bottomless night,

shards of ice, cinder-dust, smoke—
suns that never stop

exploding.

UNSETTLED

From this new home I watch the street: pickups, cars,
school buses, students bent beneath their backpacks,

people walking dogs, coming from the store,
the mail man, cyclists and joggers checking their phones.

In the yard a maple, its winged fruit hanging mothlike
in the branches, its tossing leaves shivering its pools of sky.

Yesterday I drove a thousand miles to get here,
a thousand miles through horizontal rain,

through all the landscapes of the west: snow peaks,
red canyons, yellow stone, great meandering rivers,

infinitudes of desert, basin, range: white turning to
wedgwood blue; sagebrush green to blond.

Now, like a woman emptying her apron
of gathered fruit, this day has opened—

a morning lit with birdsong, walking the forest,
dogwood soaking shadows, water combing stone.

At home, purple iris bowing over the footpath, gardens
frothing with blossoms—apple, cherry, magnolia.

The shadow of a tiny bird rolls sideways
over the lawn and suddenly I want to cry:

the place I've lived in up 'til now, far away,
still under snow, barren of the first, sweet pricks of green,

its great and empty landscapes vast enough for elk,
for buffalo—herds of them—wild enough for grizzlies—

animals these days unheard of here:
why this day, so full of sunshine and of flowers,

cannot console me.

IN THE CITY

*Why give us the memory of flying—
and make us without wings?*

Here there is only stone and filth,
the sound of sirens whining.

All I've ever wanted—flowers,
the wild, the fingers of the wind

along my skin—a forgotten
painting left out in the rain.

Yet even here, like a secret lover's
eyes, occasionally it beckons:

flash of wing through
the cloud-smeared sky,

a hovering of light on
the western horizon,

a fallen fence, trash spread
through the garden,

hives upended, apples
ripped from their trees.

Hollow-boned with longing
I watch the pellucid sky

searching for its
traceless shadow.

Christine Mulvey (www.christinemulvey.com) was born and raised in Ireland in 1957. She spent the first half of her life as an educator, activist and community organizer, working primarily with women.

At the age of forty, drawn by the beauty of wild nature and by its power to feed, heal and inspire, she moved alone to Montana. There she spent time cavorting with bison, wolves, grizzly bears and wild places and also began to write poetry, short stories, memoir and a novel. She now lives in Northern California with her husband, Jack, her dog and her two cats, exulting in the company of tall trees, year-round flowers and the majesty of the Pacific Ocean.

She has studied with Marie Howe, Jane Hirshfield, Joe Millar, Dorianne Laux and Ellen Bass. Her first Chapbook *The Bruise of Your Absence* was published by Finishing Line Press in 2020. Her memoir *Mine To Carry: An Irishwoman's Journey Through Forbidden Pregnancy,* won Grand Prize in the North Street Book Prize in 2020. Her novel *A Dream of Flying* is forthcoming. Her poems have appeared in a number of literary journals, including the NAUGATUK RIVER REVIEW, the WHITEFISH REVIEW, MOBIUS, LAST NIGHT and the online Poetry Journal WOMEN'S VOICES FOR CHANGE.

www.ingramcontent.com/pod-product-compliance
Lightning Source LLC
LaVergne TN
LVHW041602070426
835507LV00011B/1257